HOW TO IMAGINE
STEPS FOR A BETTER, HAPPIER LIFE

Kfir Luzzatto, Ph.D., Dip. Hyp.

Pine Ten, LLC
205 N Michigan Ave.
Chicago, IL 60601

The author of this book does not dispense medical advice or prescribe the use of any technique as a form of treatment for physical, emotional or medical problems without the advice of a physician, either directly or indirectly. The intent of the author is only to offer information of a general nature. In the event that you use any of the information in this book for yourself, which is your constitutional right, the author and the publisher assume no responsibility for your actions.

First publication, February 2020

Copyright © 2020 by Kfir Luzzatto.

All rights reserved. No part of this book may be used or reproduced in any form without permission, except as provided by U.S. Copyright Law. For information, please address Pine Ten, LLC.

ISBN: 978-1-938212-86-4

Table of Contents

Foreword by Adam Eason 1

Introduction 5

CHAPTER 1: Why Imagination Matters 8
    Our Obsession with Imagination 10
    Analogical Reasoning 11
    Imagination and Empathy 12

CHAPTER 2: Imagination and Memory 14
    Memories Can Be Manipulated 16
    False Bad Memories 17
    Rewriting Your Memories 18

CHAPTER 3: What Imagination Can Do 21

CHAPTER 4: When to Imagine and How 25
    Building Your Imagery 26
    Morning Twilight Dreaming 27
    Evening Twilight Dreaming 28
    Daydreaming 30

CHAPTER 5: Imagination and Dreams 33
    Influencing Our Dreams 35
    Holding On to a Dream 37

CHAPTER 6: Imagining For Happiness 39
    Mixed Memory Reconstruction 42

Usefully Faulty 43

Prophylactic Happiness Work 44

CHAPTER 7: Imagining for Pleasure and Entertainment ... 45

Aerial View 46

Augmented Recall 47

CHAPTER 8: Imagining for Problem-Solving 49

One Way to Overcome Problem-Related Anxiety 50

Structured Problem Solving 51

A Problem-Solving Procedure 52

CHAPTER 9: Imagining For Creativity 54

Creating the House of Your Dreams 56

Putting Words Together 56

CHAPTER 10: The Fear of Imagination 58

Stopping Imagined Fear 59

Testing New Situations 60

Avoiding Overdoing It 61

CHAPTER 11: Conclusion 63

Meet the Author: 66

Other Non-Fiction Books by Kfir Luzzatto 67

Appendix A:

The Pleasures of Imagination Defended, 1889 68

Appendix B:

Using Still Images to Recreate a Movie 69

Foreword

Crossing the finish line of the longest endurance running event I ever seriously competed in, and the lifting of the heaviest weight I ever competitively lifted were both events I had imagined. Such future memory creation is a process that has formed part of every training regimen I have undergone for any sport I have excelled at. The process is one I encourage so many to get comfortable with and add to one's set of mental skills and my professional experience has shown me that elite athletes tend to engage their imagination regularly and harness it to advance their sporting performance.

Whenever we successfully achieve something that we planned, it always makes everything feel so worthwhile and therefore becoming familiar with that experience before it has happened in reality makes sense. Why are more people not making this a natural part of their own training, or of their own lives?

These good feelings generate passion for the goal. I imagine the satisfaction of (my personal interpretation of) success, the glow of accomplishment and that satisfaction serves as a real motivation, a passion for achievement that offers me additional sustenance throughout the plan of moving towards the goal.

This is one small example of a vast number of varying other ways of what we can do with our imagination when we learn how to use it better.

Here in the laboratory of Bournemouth University on the South Coast of England, we teach standardised self-hypnosis protocols and imagination skills to research participants to measure how they can and do influence an individual's perceptions, how they can advance the ability to perform a range of cognitive tasks and even how they can be used to increase physical strength. Two things stand out from my researcher experience:

1. How incredibly powerful the imagination is and how much it can influence our experience of life;

2. How alien it is for a great many people to attempt to advance one's imagination skills (often leading to the realisation that one was not making best use of the imagination previously).

Kfir Luzzatto was an exceptional student of mine and is today a graduate of my college. I write "exceptional" because of the seeming ease and speed by which he achieved a very high level of academic understanding but also how he linked ideas together and found solutions to problems. When we spoke to discuss his coursework, it was clear how much stimulation he derived from his studies and his enjoyment of being a student learning new things were undoubtedly fuelled by the long-established talents he already had. As an accomplished author of fiction, Kfir has spent hundreds of hours stimulating the imaginations of his readers; shaping great mindscapes, engaging them in twisting plots, creating emotional shifts and developing the readers relationships with characters. It made complete sense to me therefore that he should combine and synergise this ability to stimulate the imagination with his in-depth studies and academic exploration resulting in this book.

The world and our lives can pretty much always benefit from the increasingly effective use of imagination. We all possess the limitless potential of an imagination. To some, imaginative creativity is about making new connections—and that is literally physiologically true within our neurology. Creativity is the mind's growing edge. It often involves a lot of discovery. By creating new connections, you build your brain power and develop mental and interpersonal flexibility, which can begin to heighten your ability to do a huge array of things with more and more ease. Imagine this (albeit metaphorically): every time you link two things together, you create a third entity. That new connection can itself then connect with other ideas, additional possibilities. Imagine the impact this can have in your imagination and throughout a system such as your brain. This book's creation illustrates this beautifully and this book is about to do the same for you.

Your imagination can play a great role and offer much value in your life. In the modern world your imagination can even be the most valuable resource you have. Researchers who tracked brain activity of freestyle rappers showed that the parts of the brain that we use in "business as usual" thinking are totally switched off when we are being creative, whereas other parts of our mind that we do not use every day are quite active. Now is your time to reactivate.

When you follow the instructions in this book, your renewed imagination will help you renew the curiosity and sense of awe you experienced as a child discovering the world around you. You'll enable yourself to view the world through a fresh set of eyes. You'll get to know yourself again and better, you'll value quiet time where you'll get to consciously and purposefully tap into your imagination and learn how to use it more effectively.

"Imagination is the beginning of creation. You imagine what you desire, you will what you imagine, and at last, you create what you will." —— George Bernard Shaw

Read, apply and enjoy this book.

Adam Eason
Author of *The Science of Self-Hypnosis*

Introduction

Imagine how you would feel if, most of the time, you forgot to use your arm to pick up objects and only occasionally moved it from side to side. It would atrophy, and after a while, you would find it hard to lift even the lightest of weights.

That's the equivalent of what you are doing to your imagination.

The power of imagination is intensely discussed in New Age books, as well as in academic writing on subjects such as religion, psychology, hypnosis, and creativity. But we seem to have forgotten the impact of imagination—or, rather, of the lack of its utilization—on our everyday life. Imagination is the most powerful, yet underutilized resource that we have, and because we neglect it, our happiness and well-being suffer unnecessarily.

This book aims to relieve its readers of common misconceptions, so they can make better use of their imagination, to feel better and happier. You will find that it is a light, result-oriented read, which unlocks tools you already have, without engaging in deep discussions of philosophic or otherwise profound matters.

But why am I explaining all this, when I can actually show it to you? You can easily get a taste of the power of your imagination and the control you have over it. Read the following paragraphs, follow the instructions, and judge for yourself. **Even better:** Listen to a recording of the instructions by going to https://www.doitwithwords.com/recording or by scanning the QR Code:

"Turn off the ring on your phone. Make sure that the room is quiet, not too cold or too hot, and the light is not too bright. Sit in a comfortable chair and close your eyes. Take stock of your mood. Are you tense or tired? Just acknowledge your sensations, whatever they are.

Take two deep breaths. Now imagine that you are lying on soft cushions in a small wooden boat, near the shore of a quiet, blue mountain lake. The lake is surrounded by tall trees and by lush vegetation. Keep your eyes closed and feel the rays of the sun on your face and the gentle, cooling breeze on your body. Feel them. Good!

Now let a broad smile spread across your face for a moment. Enjoy the scene that you have just created. You deserve it.

You hear the chirping birds and the rustle of the tree leaves in the wind. Listen to them carefully for a few moments. Inhale deeply and smell the sweet scent of the blooming flowers.

The boat is rocked from side to side by the gentle flux of the lake waters. Let it lull you and enjoy the soothing sensations it brings. Feel how you are deeply relaxed by the pleasant sounds of nature, the clean air, and the sweet scent of flowers that you can almost taste in your mouth.

Enjoy this pleasant sensation for a minute or two. Bask in it. When you're ready, open your eyes and return to the present."

I don't need to ask you if you feel better now than before. I know you do. If you were tense, you are now more relaxed, and your mood has improved. That's what you can do for yourself if you invest only a few minutes of your time. So imagine what you will be able to accomplish after you learn more.

If you want to explore the power of your own imagination and discover how it can improve your daily life and make you happier, keep reading.

CHAPTER 1
Why Imagination Matters

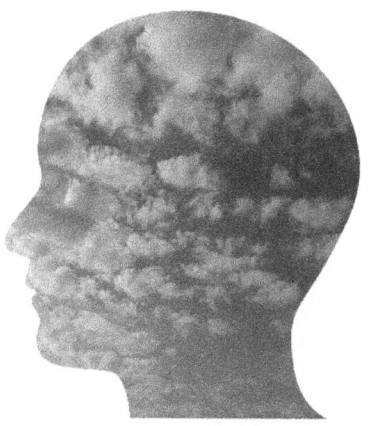

Imagining is not the same as being delusional. There are two types of imaginative processes: Active and Passive. In fact, we imagine all the time, passively, which in many cases does us no good. Passive imagination is often driven by wrong cognitions, fueled by misinterpretation, stress, and fear. Assume, for instance, that you are participating in some important competition (for instance, for a job or academic studies), and the website to which you submitted your forms states that, "typically," your submission will be responded to in 10–15 days. It is now day 15, and you have not heard back from them. You start to run the "most possible" reasons for this in your head:

1. You didn't fill in the forms correctly, and the submission was ignored.

2. You didn't click the "upload" button, and your application was never actually submitted.

3. You made a typo in your email address and missed a deadline that was sent to you.

You get the idea. Panic, of course, ensues, as you go through this list, imagining and visualizing all these terrible possible situations. The fact that the next day you receive a positive response will not immunize you against your passive imagination, which will make you miserable again at the next opportunity.

"Active imagination" (a term coined by the famous psychiatrist C. G. Jung) is your antidote to many such situations. It allows you to create a realistic picture of the events that are likely to develop and even to savor the hoped-for positive result (thus avoiding sleepless nights and a tense refreshing of your inbox at five-minute intervals during the day), while allowing you to prepare yourself for the (hopefully remote) case that the outcome will not be the one you are hoping for.

Active imagination will also help you to prepare for bad times, by helping you visualize yourself going through the expected plight and examine in detail various ways to deal with it. It also permits you to analyze your feelings toward each variant of the expected situation. When the bad times actually arrive, you are much better prepared for them if you invested in active imagination, than if you let your passive imagination run wild.

Active imagination has many other roles, all of which can help you to feel better, happier and more optimistic, and achieve your goals faster and more effectively. I will address those in detail in the following chapters.

Our Obsession with Imagination

At the time of writing this book, I ran a search for the word "imagination" in PubMed.gov (the US National Library of Medicine of the National Institutes of Health), and came up with 31,261 scientific papers! Those range from psychologic observations to brain scans; they explore the whole gamut of areas in which our imagination matters, and most authors agree that there is a lot of exploring yet to be done. But the basic fact—that human beings have a tremendous ability to imagine and do not utilize it nearly enough—still remains.

Scientific research is of course important, but it doesn't really help ordinary people, who are not likely to have their brain scans taken, because (like in many other fields of research) the literature treats the concept of "imagination" in a very specialized and scientific manner, hence making it less relevant for the layman. I have made it a life goal to take abstruse subjects and make them more approachable for the general public; one of the reasons for my resolve to study and qualify as a clinical hypnotherapist was my urge to gain a deeper understanding of what makes people tick. Digging deeper connected many dots for me but also made me realize that we ignore easily available, simple tools like imagination, although they are within everybody's grasp.

Above everything else, imagination is what permits us to function. Before we operate a new machine, after learning its parts and its various functions, we imagine how it should operate and what will happen when we turn it on. True, in most cases, that will be only a rough approximation of what will actually happen. We may be surprised that the noise the contraption makes is louder than expected or that a light suddenly comes on, of the existence of which we were not aware, but we will use the imagined event to initiate our learning process and correct our image of the machine's functioning as we learn more. In contrast, now imagine (no pun intended) that you approach a humongous machine without taking the time to consider what it will do when you push the "start" button. If the machine has moving parts and is loud, you may be in for a shock.

Kahneman[1] explains that imaginability plays an important role in the evaluation of probabilities in real-life situations. The risk involved in an adventurous expedition, for example, is evaluated by imagining contingencies with which the expedition is not equipped to cope. If many such difficulties are vividly portrayed, the expedition can be made to appear exceedingly dangerous, although the ease with which disasters are imagined need not reflect their actual likelihood. Conversely, the risk involved in an undertaking may be grossly underestimated if some possible dangers are either difficult to conceive of or simply do not come to mind.

Analogical Reasoning

When faced with the unknown, we try to understand it using analogical reasoning. If some years ago we were bitten by a big, bad dog where it hurts, when confronted again with a lookalike of that dog, we are likely to reach the conclusion that we are in danger of being bitten again, which will activate our fight-or-flight (or, in this case, flight-and-flight) response. This is different from someone who has become phobic of dogs in

---

[1] Kahneman, Daniel. ***Thinking, Fast and Slow*** (p. 426). Farrar, Straus and Giroux.

general, after having been bitten, for whom the fight-or-flight mechanism may be automatically activated, regardless of what the dog looks like.

This new dog may be a mild, gentle one, who has no intention whatsoever to bite us, but our reaction will probably be a reasonable one, under the circumstances. So, how did we apply analogical reasoning to that situation? 1) We remembered the bad, biting dog; 2) we decided that this one reminds us of it; and 3) we imagined (whether consciously or sub-consciously) this new dog biting us. If we had our imagination mechanism removed, we would never be able to use analogical reasoning, which is a precious tool that we must use if we want to stay alive and well.

Imagination and Empathy
Imagination also plays a critical part in human interaction. For instance, a 1997 paper[2] suggests that it is at least partially the activity of the moral imagination, which allows the sensitive nurse or doctor to perceive non-verbal cues and attend to patients sufficiently, to know when the patient is capable of coping with bad news, rather than merely stating such news in a cold, factual way, without any attempt to consider if the time is ripe.

This boils down to empathy—if you cannot put yourself in the other person's shoes (i.e., imagine what he or she is going through), you will never be able to feel or show empathy.

These are just examples of how our imagination constantly works for us, in a passive way. I need to give you a little more background, and then we'll start seeing how we can use our imagination actively and reap surprising benefits. But before we do that, a quick flashback will provide some perspective.

---

[2] P. Anne Scott, *Journal of Medical Ethics* 1997; 23: 45-50.

Many things that were clearly understood centuries ago seem to have become less clear to us nowadays. Before our modern times, people had much more time on their hands that they had to fill. There was no TV, Facebook, or Twitter and their like, to steal precious time from them, so their imagination played a greater role than nowadays. It is useful to realize how things were when life was simpler, and for that reason I have included as Appendix A, a short article titled **The Pleasures of Imagination Defended**, published on September 7, 1889 in the British magazine **THE HOSPITAL**, which reports the words of Sir James Crichton Browne in his address to the British Medical Association, a snippet of which is reported below:

"... *to the healthy minded, imaginative literature may heighten happiness, afford solace in suffering and sorrow, give brace to exertion, and lessen the sense of fatigue. ... The insane are the least imaginative of beings, the lunatic is as dull as a stone, and idiocy is the absolute negation of imagination.*"

I couldn't have put it better myself.

CHAPTER 2
Imagination and Memory

A long time ago the popular belief was that each event we live is memorized and stored in the meanders of our brain, whence it is retrieved when needed, by "calling for it." This simplistic model assumes that the memory of an event is fixed, and while we may have trouble recalling it, once we are able to do so we will always be faced with the same memory. But this model is wrong.

What happens when a memory is created, is the generation of a pattern of neural activity that was originally generated in response to a particular event, echoing the brain's perception of the real event. During memory recall, the brain "replays" that pattern of neural activity. In fact, there is no real, solid distinction between the act of remembering and the act of thinking, and since actively imagining involves thinking, there is also no distinction between the act of remembering and the act of imagining. A 2015 work[3] strengthened the conclusion that the part of our brain responsible for recalling memories is the hippocampus, but that is also where our imagination operates, at least in part.

Okay, I hear you complaining that this is getting a bit too scientific and that I promised this book would not turn into an exercise in neuroscience, but please bear with me a little longer, and you'll soon see the point. I am insisting on this issue, because later on we are going to learn how to put the fallacy of our recollection system to good use, so it is important that we recognize it.

Put simply, our brain pieces together the various modalities of the memory (images, sounds, taste, smell, etc.) and, as the authors of this work point out, the encoding and retrieval process will be as error prone as any other cognitive function. One can falsely "recollect" with high confidence. Put in plain English, this means that the memory we recall may be wrong in part or entirely (more on this later).

The connection between the memory and imaginative processes is important. Other authors[4] have pointed out that when people recall episodic memories and imagined fictitious

---

[3] Aidan J. Horner et al., **NATURE COMMUNICATIONS** | 6:7462 | DOI: 10.1038/ncomms8462

[4] Peter Zeidman and Eleanor A. Maguire, **Nat Rev Neurosci.** 2016 Mar; 17(3): 173–182.

events set in the past or future, there is a part of the hippocampus (located in our brain) that is significantly engaged with imagination, which is part of a larger region activated during both imagination and recall. (The anatomic details are really not that important here, however.)

Memories Can Be Manipulated

Humans are obsessed with their own pasts. A large part of our conscious mental lives is spent reminiscing about past experiences and sharing those experiences with others. However, now that we know that "recalling" and "imagining" are closely related processes and that the recalling process is inherently faulty, how do we know which of our memories are "true memories" and which are false memories, the fruit of our imagination? One can (even accurately) imagine a past event, which one believes to have occurred.[5] This is, in fact, common when we represent events of which we have only second-hand information, the so-called "vicarious memories" (i.e., recollections of events that happened to other people).

It has certainly happened to you that a single small detail—a few bars of a song, a smell, a taste, or a word—caused a memory to suddenly pop up in your mind, complete with details relating to events, people, and surroundings. But how accurate is the picture that it has evoked for you? You have no means to know, although if it is a very old memory, such as one of something that happened when you were very young, I would not bank on its accuracy. In a remarkable experiment, known as the "lost in the mall" experiment, psychologist Elizabeth Loftus proved[6] that it is possible, with little effort, to inject a complete memory of something that never happened,

---

[5] Johannes B. Mahr and Gergely Csibra, ***Behav Brain Sci.*** 2018; 41
[6] Loftus, E. F., ***American Psychologist***, 48, 518-537 (1993).

which is then remembered in great detail (in the experiment, the memory of having been lost in a mall when he was five years old was implanted in a 14-year-old boy). This is as scary as it gets.

It turns out that you do have control over your memories, which is good news, and we will discuss how to use it. Unfortunately, others also have control over it, and that is very bad news. Saul M. Kassin[7] is an expert in false confessions. He explains that innocent but vulnerable suspects, exposed to highly suggestive interrogation tactics, not only confess but come to believe they committed the crime in question.

From all this we can conclude that our imagination can strongly influence our memories. Memories are not set in stone and can be changed. When they change, our reality changes, because we have no way to tell whether a more accurate memory should be recalled instead.

False Bad Memories

Now assume that you have created a bad memory that does not accurately reflect your reality. Or maybe it does, but it is not serving you well ...

I had a memory that tormented me for decades. In my early teens I met an old woman, Angela was her name, who lived near my home. She was a widow, very poor and lonely. For a year or so I used to visit her frequently, to help her with simple chores and keep her company. At last, her health faltered; she no longer had the strength to live alone and decided to move to a hospice. I had this haunting memory of her, leaving her house for the last time, with a small suitcase that held all her belongings. I recalled her gazing at me reproachfully, as if to imply it my fault that she had to leave, because I was unable to support her sufficiently;

---

[7] Saul M. Kassin, **CURRENT DIRECTIONS IN PSYCHOLOGICAL SCIENCE**, Volume 17—Number 4, 2008

and the memory of me, unable to find words to console her, was very vivid. I think that I truly felt guilty that I hadn't helped her more, so she could stay where she had lived all her life. This memory came back to me on many occasions, for instance when looking at an old photograph taken on our street or smelling rosemary chicken (the heavenly dish she cooked and often prepared when she knew I was coming).

The only problem is that this was a false memory.

Many years later this woman came up in conversation with my mother, and it turned out that she remembered the event quite differently (I had completely forgotten that she was there too). In her recollection, Angela had been anything but reproachful—on the contrary, she had gone on and on about how much I had helped her, and how sorry she was to let me down and go away. For whatever reason, I had chalked her leaving up to my own failure, and ruminating on it had created the false piece of memory. I probably thought that I was to blame and imagined the reaction I deserved.

The revelation that my recollection of the event was wrong initiated a chain reaction. I trusted my mother's memory more than mine—after all, I was a young boy then. This helped me to correct my memory almost immediately. I simply relived the event in my imagination just as my mother had told it, and that was it. No more pangs of guilt when I smelled rosemary.

Rewriting Your Memories

It didn't take me long to understand the implications of this process and the opportunities it offers. These are limitless and with a little planning can be applied to a variety of incorrect memories. But, of course, I haven't discovered anything new. The process, called Imagery Rescripting in the scientific literature,[8] is well known and has many applications. It is a therapeutic technique addressing specific memories of earlier experiences associated with present problems. By imagining that the course of events is changed in a more desired direction, powerful therapeutic effects have been found, even in addressing Post-Traumatic Stress Disorder (PTSD).[9]

Imagery Rescripting is used by specialized therapists in various ways and is not a method actually known or available to the general public. However, there is a do-it-yourself (DIY) version of this method, which anybody can do, following the example recounted above. If you replay a memory and smooth its corners, either by placing a somewhat different interpretation on matters or by viewing the course of the events unfold differently—in most cases, as you would have liked them to unfold or, as you now understand, better reflects what actually transpired—chances are that it will become a less-troubling or more pleasant memory.

I am not advocating kidding yourself into believing that a memory is completely different from what really happened; I am merely suggesting giving events, sensations, and images connected with the event a different shade. Often, we remember events in black-and-white terms, particularly if they involved confrontation or anger. When we revisit them in a calmer state of mind, we are able to see that there may be lighter shades of gray to it. We do that many times, for instance, simply by reconsidering what happened and debating whether we didn't overreact. However, this reflective practice works much better if we can incorporate it in the movie that our imagination is creating while rescripting the events.

To learn how to actually go about doing this, read on to Chapter 4.

---

[8] Arntz, A., **Journal of Experimental Psychopathology**, 189–208 (2012)
[9] Satoshi Kida, ***Psychopharmacology (Berl).*** 2019; 236(1): 49–57.

CHAPTER 3
What Imagination Can Do

Passive imagination does many of the things that active imagination does but without any direction or guidance on our part. Passive imagination happens all the time and is influenced by events, the state of our health (or our perception of it), our surroundings, things we hear, and other inputs that we knowingly or unknowingly receive. Allowing ourselves to be at the mercy of our passive imagination is like boarding a boat with no oars or helm and allowing it to take us through tumultuous waters, all the while hoping for the best.

Passive imagination is the culprit in some of our most insidious issues. If we are apprehensive—either because circumstances make us so or because that is our nature—we are likely to catastrophize, reaching potentially unbearable levels of stress. To catastrophize "properly," we need to let our imagination run wild, showing us frightening scenarios, which most likely will never happen and statistically are even not remotely likely to happen. However, at this point the damage has already been done, as our blood pressure and other ailments will prove in the long run.

The activities suggested in this book have no therapeutic purpose (although one might argue that simply feeling happier is therapeutic in itself). In psychotherapy, use is made of effective, specialized techniques, all using imagination as a tool, which may help us to deal with different issues. Those are not to be confused with the make-feel-good procedures suggested in the following chapters. There is much we can do ourselves to improve our well-being when we don't have an issue that requires specialized help. Moreover, if and when we find ourselves in need of professional help, having honed our ability to use our imagination on a daily basis will serve us very well to achieve better and faster results.

To better understand what the specialized techniques that we are not going to need for the purpose of this book are, the following are examples:

Meditation: I hesitated whether meditation should be included in this list, because, properly speaking, this technique does not exploit our active imagination. Although many meditative techniques exist, and I don't pretend to cover them all in this brief note, the most common meditative practices have as their aim to stop us from imagining for a while; but imagination is still a central factor in it, so here it is. When meditating, we fix our mind on something trivial like our breath, and if thoughts cross our mind, we simply note them and let them go. This procedure quiets our mind, and if we are stressed, for example, we stop our troubling trend of thought, thus easing our stress.

Guided Imagery: Guided imagery is mostly associated with healing. Mental imagery can be used to achieve deep physiologic relaxation, stimulate healing responses in your body, and create an inner dialogue that can help you better understand your health and what you can do to improve it. According to Dr. Martin Rossman,[10] a well-known practitioner in the field, guided imagery can be helpful, though not always curative, in 90 percent of the problems that people bring to a primary-care doctor.

It is worth noting that guided imagery plays an important role also in hypnosis and in neuro-linguistic programming (NLP), and this should not surprise us, since as should be clear by now, imagination is central to our life.

Hypnosis: Hypnosis (including self-hypnosis) is another technique that relies heavily on the subject's imagination. As opposed to guided imagery, hypnosis is not limited to direct suggestion of useful imagery and is capable of exploiting our imagination also in other ways, using indirect suggestions and metaphors; but the "engine of change," the mechanism that will achieve the desired outcome, is still fueled by our imagination. Because of the powerful techniques that can be used, hypnosis is capable of creating quick changes in the way in which we perceive ourselves and our body, including our physical

---

[10] Rossman, Martin L., ***Guided Imagery for Self-Healing***, New World Library.

perception, for instance, of pain. Accordingly, its therapeutic usefulness is substantially greater than that of other imagination-based techniques.

Neuro-Linguistic Programming (NLP): Simply put, NLP assumes that each person makes a definite map of the world in his or her mind, based on his senses, which map may be more or less different from objective reality. Different people have different maps of the world and experience their lives and make decisions according to those maps. Our own thoughts are responsible for how we feel and behave, from which it follows that we must have the ability to control them. NLP gives us many effective techniques to help us control our thoughts and change our emotional state. All NLP techniques require that you use your imagination, according to specific steps and stages.

All these techniques (and a few that I am not mentioning) aim at creating a change in our perception, when we run into a more or less acute problem that makes us realize that we need "to do something" about it. What I will do in the next pages, instead, is to show you how we can improve the quality of our life and particularly our level of happiness. We want to do that *before* we feel that we have a problem—in fact, **when we do not have "a problem" at all**, except the daily ones that everybody has. We are normally unable to link those daily issues to a level of content that is lower than that to which we are entitled. By fostering our level of content, we will prevent many of the issues that may prove more difficult and troublesome to resolve, once they have incubated in our mind and body for a long time.

CHAPTER 4
When to Imagine and How

Once you have actively imagined for a while, you will no longer need to make any special preparations to reach what I will term here "an imaginative mindset," and you will be able to actively imagine everywhere and at any time. Nevertheless, while you are in the earlier stages of flexing your imaginative muscles and honing your imaginative skills, you will find it useful to create an environment that facilitates your work. I will address that later in this chapter. However, at least twice a day you will naturally be in a state that requires no preparation to use your active imagination beneficially: during *"twilight dreaming"* (don't google the term; I have just coined it).[11]

Twilight dreaming may occur in two different situations, which I will treat separately below, but let's look first at how to work with imagination.

Building Your Imagery

Regardless of when you practice imagination, your imagery must have motion in it. It is not enough to see a beautifully realistic picture. At a minimum, it must move and have sound and preferably also any other sensation that you can put into it, including touch, smell, and taste. Once you have the basic image, you need to let it become a movie. You are the movie director and will decide which way it is going, how fast it should play, if and when it should rewind to allow you to relive a particularly important moment, and so on.

You should start by taking a close look at the basic image, which will become the first frame in your movie. Take the time to analyze it, see its colors, hear its sounds, and, as much as you can, use other senses: smell and touch. Once you have examined the image in detail, consider the feeling it conveys to you. Does it make you sad, happy, relaxed? Next, imagine two or three more frames of the movie; see how the image changes when you go forward, then go back to the first frame, and let it animate itself. Having a few more frames already at hand will help the flow of the movie, and your imagination will naturally fill the gaps between frames.

Because you are your scriptwriter, you have complete control over your movie. However, it is important to let your imagination do some of the work by itself, to the extent that the

---

[11] Twilight dreaming is not "lucid dreaming" (a dream during which dreamers are aware they are dreaming), or "active dreaming" (a new-age concept completely extraneous to active imagination).

movie doesn't have to be completely scripted; it must evolve "on the fly." You will have a rough idea of what you want to happen in it, but unless it takes a turn that bothers you, don't try to stop it from going in an unexpected direction. You may learn a lot from where the story goes, if you avoid being a control freak and instead give your imagination some latitude.

Creating your own movie from a basic imagery is a skill you will learn very easily if you don't have it already (many of us unconsciously do that at times), but by using active imagination, you will create better, more interesting, and even fascinating movies that have the consistency of reality.

Now let's talk about *when* you should do all that.

Morning Twilight Dreaming
The first opportunity for twilight dreaming is when you wake up in the morning, particularly if your awakening is a gentle, natural one. If you are awoken abruptly by a loud alarm clock or a screaming child, that opportunity may be lost. You can easily learn to allow the feeling of mild confusion, which is natural when emerging from sleep, to linger long enough for you to turn your mind to pleasant thoughts—but not just thoughts: images. Say, for instance, that you particularly enjoy walking in the park. Imagine yourself there, walking around, breathing the clean air, feeling the sun rays on your skin, listening to the early morning birds, and you may be surprised at the great feeling with which you will begin your day, carrying those pleasant images with you for a while.

But your imagery does not have to be limited to soothing and pleasant scenarios: you can use it to prepare for your day in a more specific way. For example, let's assume that you are scheduled to give a presentation at work to an audience with which you are not familiar. You are obviously worried lest you make mistakes, forget some important point, or express yourself unclearly. Maybe this has been worrying you in the back of your mind for days. So what you do now is imagine yourself giving the presentation. Make it a movie in your mind, and if you hit a difficult point, rewind it and do it again and again, until you feel confident that you are doing it right. Make sure to include your audience in your imagery; see how they are pleased with what you are saying and how they react positively. I will bet you any sum that your presentation will go way better than it would have if you simply jumped out of bed when you opened your eyes and went to work.

The options for exploiting this moment of your morning are endless. You may relive a pleasant memory or anticipate an upcoming pleasant event. You can just create an imaginary event to explore a situation that is not real for you but which you find appealing. You can imagine yourself parachuting out of an airplane or lying on a secluded beach with a good drink. That's what is great about imagination: it has no limits and it frees you, even if for a short time, from the bonds of real life, allowing you to experience things that are not within your practical reach.

Evening Twilight Dreaming
You know that feeling, when you are about to fall asleep but not just sleeping yet? That mellow sensation that you will soon be in that pleasant place and are allowing yourself to sink slowly into it? That's the sensation that you want to hang on to at this point.

Evening twilight dreaming can be used for the same purposes as its morning counterpart, but it also has an important role in respect of dreaming, which I will explore in the next chapter. You can use this time to prepare for the next day or revisit an event of the day that you have not yet fully internalized. For instance, you can use it to attribute a reasonable meaning to something that another person said or did, which left you puzzled or worried. In the blessed state of evening twilight dreaming there is a clarity that you don't achieve during normal waking hours, when your mind is busy dealing with chores and outside stimuli. Events make more sense and assume less ominous meanings (unless, of course, you abandon them to your passive imagination, and then you may be in trouble).

This is a great opportunity to make peace with events that you can't change and see them leading up to less catastrophic conclusions than you envisioned when they occurred. Your reality is what informs your actions and your feelings, so it follows that if an event is beyond your control, your best option is to place it in the less-troubling context within your reality. Let's take an example.

You broke your arm, and now it is in a cast. What good is it going to do to you, if you picture yourself unable to play tennis—the game you love—in the future? But of course, this is the first thing that occurred to you at the hospital, and you insistently probed the treating doctor as to the severity of your condition, getting only noncommittal answers in response. Your arm is broken, and there is nothing you can do to unbreak it, so why break your spirit as well? Here is what you need to do: That night (and any other night of days when your broken arm bothers you), as you reach the imaginative mindset during your twilight dreaming time, imagine yourself removing the cast and finding that your arm is completely mended. Watch yourself playing tennis (carefully, please) and feeling that everything is back on track. Repeat that imagery until you no longer catastrophize about the future of your arm.

Doing the suggested imagery will fetch you two positive results: it will stop you from worrying, thus lowering your stress level, and that positive approach and lower stress may aid the healing process. I'm not pulling your leg: there is actual evidence for the importance of stress and imagery for the body's healing process.[12]

But what will happen, you ask, if after removing the cast I find that the damage is substantial, and I cannot play tennis anymore? Well, then you will have sufficient time to worry about it and look for solutions. Why worry about it before you have to and when you can't do anything about it? Since you are a rational individual, you knew all along that your hope for a full recovery was not a given result and that there may be challenges to deal with later on. You may even have cautiously explored that possibility and your reaction if that turns out to be so. That understanding will temper your disappointment.

Daydreaming

Since we have referred to the two previous windows for imagination as "twilight dreaming," for consistency I refer here to the rest of the day as "daydreaming." It is useful to find a time to use our imagination during the day, if we want to deal with thoughts, issues, and expected situations that are bothering us. However, if we are not expert at imagining, we need to prime our mind for it.

Inside: We want to sit comfortably, in a room that is not too cold or too hot, and lower the lights enough so they are not too bright or in our eyes but not so much that we incur the risk of falling asleep. Active imagination requires us to be relaxed but fully awake.

Outside: That is my favorite place to sit down and imagine. You first need to find a place where you can sit for a while with your eyes closed, without having people think that

---

[12] Jean-Philippe and Janice K. Kiecolt-Glaser, ***Crit Care Nurs Clin North Am.*** 2012 Jun; 24(2): 201–213.

you are a weirdo and skateboarding kids bumping into you. Once again, you need enough shade but not so much that you feel cold. A gentle breeze on your face is a big bonus.

Imaginative mindset: Achieving the appropriate imaginative mindset requires preparations. You must clear your mind of daily thoughts, for instance by doing a quick meditation. A simple deep breathing exercise also works, but I recommend making sure that your body is thoroughly relaxed before starting. If you are tense, any suitable relaxation method will work.

Before you begin, it is desirable to have an at least a rough idea of what situation you want to explore, but if there is no particular thing on your mind, it is also great to let an image pop up in your head spontaneously and create a movie on the fly. There may be issues that you will find beneficial imagining about, of which you are not aware, and those will find their way to your awareness by allowing them to emerge when they want to.

Some people find it necessary to start by going to a safe inner place, as is customarily done with guided imagery, which is an (of course) imaginary place that you find relaxing. Any feel-good place is fine; for example, a mountain lake, a tranquil meadow, or a path in the forest or any other beautiful natural setting, will make for a great safe inner place. But if you are a bungee instructor and find that sitting dangling your feet above a precipice soothes you, go for it. You will normally want to have more than one safe place in which to enter an imaginative mindset, from which you can choose according to your mood. That is definitely not needed during the twilight periods, but if you find it useful during daytime, there is no harm in doing it, although in my experience it may not be needed in the long run. Whichever technique you chose to get started, the important thing is to let your imagination take you where it wants to go, **as long as it is not taking you to dark places**.

If the movie you are creating in your mind is "too daring" for you, don't ever try to stifle it. It may be allowing you to do things that you have always wanted to do and is now giving you a chance to live them, which you may never get in real life. Have you always wanted to ride a motorbike, but your wife wouldn't let you? Let's see how she stops you from doing that in your head!

Imagination can act as a safety valve that allows us to live some innocent (or, even, not so innocent) fantasy that we know will never happen in real life. Instead of feeling repressed by avoiding it, we may confront such thoughts in a safe environment, which will put them in perspective. Have you always wanted to be a great speaker but don't have the ability for it? This is not something you want to share even with your nearest and dearest, lest they make fun of you. But who's keeping you from rehearsing a great speech in your head? And then, maybe, one day you will have the opportunity to deliver that speech and will be ready for it. And if not, you have kept yourself optimistic and fulfilled, if only in your imagination.

I bet that at this point you are thinking of the one thing you don't discuss with your spouse. Put a bookmark here, and go for it!

CHAPTER 5
Imagination and Dreams

Everybody occasionally experiences tumultuous nights with bad dreams. Often those dreams (or nightmares) are the result of events that we experienced during the day or in recent times, and their connection to, and influence on, our night experience is clear. More often than not, however, we do not have a full view of the extent to which our dreams disturb our sleep, because although we may have several dream cycles during any given night, we tend to remember only the last one, unless we were awoken by an exceptionally bad one in the middle of the night or woke up right after dreaming for whatever other reason. Within a single night, several stages of sleep and time-of-night effects have been found in dreams: REM (rapid eye movement) dreams and those toward the end of the night tend to become longer, as well as more vivid, emotional, and bizarre.

The question is, can we influence the way we dream? In my experience the answer is positive, although this influence is certainly limited—but not insignificant—and difficult to quantify. And here is a somewhat circular reasoning, which is nevertheless worth following: There is no clear evidence that using our imagination actively to influence our dreams actually gets the job done. All evidence is anecdotal at best. And yet, if we agree with the postulate that what matters is our perception of the world, then it doesn't really matter whether our recollection of the dream is accurate or not, as long as it provides for a more positive experience.

Melanie G. Rosen argues that[13] dream reports are often confabulated or fabricated because of poor memory, bizarre dream content, and cognitive deficits. It has been experimentally demonstrated that subjects rationalize strange elements in narratives, leaving out supernatural or bizarre components when reporting waking memories of stories.

But does that matter at all? I don't think so. If, after a few days during which we felt that our sleep was disturbed by bad dreams, we applied active imagination (in a way that I will amplify later) and woke up feeling better, more rested, and without remembering bad dreams, why should we care what actually happened during sleep? I argue that we shouldn't. We wake up happier and start our day on the right foot, and science be damned.

---

[13] Melanie G. Rosen, **Front Psychol.** 2013; 4: 514.

Nevertheless, science is not our enemy; it is just that we must use research results with a grain of salt, because getting too scientific where we need to rely on intuition, may stifle us. An important review[14] discusses critical elements of dreaming. First of all, it concludes that the process of assimilating emotional waking-life experiences during sleep and dreaming requires imaginational abilities. Importantly, according to these authors, emotional waking-life memories are preferentially activated during sleep, thus appearing in dreams, in order to assimilate these memories into the wider memory system. The emotional waking-life memories are not necessarily bad memories—they are just that: emotional. As these authors point out, while there is some evidence that particularly unusual stressful experiences such as trauma are dreamt of, other studies have shown that experiences that were incorporated into dreams were more emotional, but no more stressful, than those that were not incorporated.

Influencing Our Dreams
Using the evening twilight dreaming time for active imagination, thereby creating positive **emotional** (although imagined) memories may help us to dream better and wake up feeling more rested and in a better mood. You don't have to take my word for it, since it doesn't cost you anything to try. It may not work for you the first time, because you need to gain some experience with it, but eventually it will get results. Everybody is different and, therefore, you need to find the way to snuggle into a twilight dreaming state that feels good for you. You also need to find the imagery that will make you feel good at the given time (which may differ from the one that will work well

---

[14] Josie E. Malinowski, and Caroline L. Horton, **Front Psychol.** 2015; 6: 1132.

for you tomorrow) and the length of time that you want to go on imagining how the imaginary events will unfold. There is an element of trial and error in all this, and that is also what is exciting about it. You create your reality—or at least the reality that you want your sleep to assume. You may wake up thinking that you have taken your imagery into your dream and kept on dreaming it. This may or may not be true, but it really doesn't matter, does it? The fact that you have managed to make active changes to your perception, changes that make you feel better, is what matters. Reality, in this respect, is what you make it.

I hope you understand that what I propose is not that you should become blissfully delusional. I fully expect you to be aware throughout that the dreams you are concocting (whether in preparation for sleep or during waking hours) are fictional. They are merely a device that helps you to reposition your experience in a manner that is more in tune with your personality, and to reframe experiences that got misplaced because you didn't have the time to explore them in detail while they were happening. They may not be "fictional" in the sense that you may be replaying events that actually happened but only in the sense that you are looking at them differently than you previously remembered them. It is a critical replaying of an event that got etched in your mind in a way that is in dissonance with what you believe it should represent.

But although correcting actual memories is a useful process, active imagination is better used to prepare for new events, rearrange the map of our world (which I will address in the next chapter), and simply generate joy by doing something fun, entertaining, and unusual, which our physical self cannot do.

Holding On to a Dream

Morning twilight dreaming can help you hold on to a great feeling that would otherwise be lost. Everybody has experienced the regret of waking up in the midst of a wonderful dream that he or she wishes would not end. You were just about to do something you really like and never have an opportunity to do, or in your dream you had started a conversation with a long-lost significant person, or you simply had an exceptionally feel-good dream, and waking up has wrecked it all. Well, it doesn't have to. If you are experienced at morning twilight dreaming, you can simply pick up the dream where it ended and keep running with it.

The trick is to avoid waking up completely. I know this is a bit vague, so I'll try to explain. You have a few seconds before the dream fades away, to do the right thing. The wrong thing, of course, is to open your eyes and make contact with reality as defined by your room and the objects in it. Once you do that, the moment is gone, so you need to make a conscious decision in those few seconds, to fight consciousness, which is trying to pull you out of your dream, and let the dream go on. You need to force the next frame of the movie forward, and then the rest will follow for as long as you are able to refuse to give in to wakefulness. One way to do that is to replay the last few "frames" of the dream, the events that developed just before you realized that you were about to wake up.

This is a good place to explain again what I mean by the term "frame" in the context of active imagination. Think of your dream (or anything you are actively imagining) as a movie. Simply put, a frame is an image in which "change happens." It doesn't have to be something huge. If you were talking to somebody, the last word or few words they uttered will define a frame. If there was movement, like you jumping aboard a train, then your foot leaving the platform will define a frame. So, in this example, if the last image in the dream (before you realized that you were waking up) was that of you after you boarded the train, go back to the platform and replay the last few frames of the dream that took you there. Doing that anchors your dream in your present consciousness and allows you to run with it, in spite of the fact that you are no longer asleep.

If you are capable of capturing your dream, you will start your day feeling happier and without the feeling of loss that will follow you when you know that you were blessed with a good dream and let it slip through your fingers.

CHAPTER 6
Imagining For Happiness

"Happiness is a habit – cultivate it."
~ Elbert Hubbard

"Very little is needed to make a happy life. It is all within YOURSELF in your way of thinking."
~ Marcus Aurelius

"Most people are about as happy as they make up their minds to be."
~ Abraham Lincoln

Facts are facts, and either we can change their impact, or we can't. If we can't change one, then we must give it the proper weight and meaning, so we don't make ourselves miserable to no useful end. Imagination can help us to reevaluate our facts, assign them their proper meaning, and view them in the appropriate perspective. Think of it as a tool that manipulates the meaning of our memories, which is akin to using Photoshop to give a picture a softer lighting and a more pleasant tint. In so treating our understanding of our memories, we can elevate our level of happiness.

This reevaluation process is not a one-shot thing and is not something we should be doing on large-scale issues. Rather, it is a process that we should integrate in our daily existence so we can undertake to correctly position all elements of our happiness as they present themselves to us, instead of postponing the heavy lifting to a time of crisis. This is so imagination can contribute to our happiness in two ways:

- by helping us to limit or eliminate bad feelings arising from events or situations that displease us; and
- rejoice in the little, positive things of our life.

As we grow older, our tendency toward depression grows too. Some of it is due to the simple realization of our age and some to biological factors like cognitive and hormonal changes. These may insidiously crawl into our perception of how happy we are and work to make us ... well, less happy. Whatever the reason for it, we can fight it. I am not talking about severe, clinical depression, mind you. That is a condition that must be treated by a mental specialist and may well need drugs to remedy a biochemical imbalance that has occurred for whatever reason. What I am referring to is what is sometimes called "the blues"; you know, when you want to eat in silence and go sulk somewhere your family won't bother you. You normally don't know to what you should attribute this mood swing, which may be a sudden one, so you will say to yourself that it's the change of weather, or that you are simply tired and want to be left alone, or any other excuse that you make yourself believe.

The truth is that it doesn't really matter what caused "the blues"—you need to fight them, simply by realizing that you don't want to be in that place. If you react quickly enough, then you'll pull yourself out of it in no time; but if you let it stew, it may require a lot more work to get over it.

So what should you do? You need to come up with an imagery to which you can relate right then and start your "movie" running on the basis of it. The imagery must be appropriate for your mood, otherwise you may find it difficult to work with it. It can be a pleasant imagery (but not too relaxing, because relaxation may depress you more) or a funny one. It doesn't matter. Anything that you can "jump on" and be carried away by, from the place where you currently are, will work.

If you have practiced active imagination for a while, you will have a stock of "movies" that you have created. It is useful to pick one of them and run with it, allowing it to branch into any direction that feels natural to you at the specific time. At other times you want to confront what is ruining your mood and take it head on by creating an appropriate imagery on the fly. That may be the case, for instance, if you have a tendency to brood over things that are lost to you forever, such as things that you once considered trivial and within your grasp. That this practice is useful is supported by research,[15] which reports a phenomenon known as "affective adaptation," the processes whereby affective responses weaken after one or more exposures to emotional events.

---

[15] Wilson, Timothy D., and Daniel T. Gilbert. 2008. **Perspectives on Psychological Science,** 3(5): 370-386.

I know people who are miserable because they can no longer lift weights like they used to. According to that approach I should be miserable because I can no longer go rock climbing as I did when I was younger—but I am not. Do I miss it? Of course I do but not as much as somebody who doesn't have my imagination, and I don't let it ruin my day.

Mixed Memory Reconstruction
Sometimes you want to relive an experience for which you only have shreds of memory. You know that whatever your imagination concocts will not be accurate, but you still need it to work. In such cases you need to use information extraneous to the event, to help you connect the dots, and you don't have to feel bad about it. Say to yourself that you are aware that most of it may well be pure fantasy, but nevertheless it will serve you well if it helps you to capture *the true feeling of the event*. In other words, the details need not be accurate to recreate for you the sensation that is connected to that experience, and your flimsy neural paths will signal to you that this is so when "the penny drops" and the sensation you were grasping for courses through your body or your mind.

Just the other day I happened to skim through a photo album. I saw this picture of myself (with much more hair than

today), tired but happy at the top of a mountain (I'm the good-looking one on the right).

The next thing I did was to gather some false detail (explained below), lean back, close my eyes, and recall the memory of that climb. In my imagination, I went through the various parts of the climb (at least, the ones I could remember) and **relived the experience**. I recalled the emotions and, surely, while I did so I embellished them a bit, but who's in my head to censor me? That brought a broad smile to my face. I felt blessed that I had had the opportunity to conquer that mountain and never for a second felt any regret. I put that event in the correct perspective of time and age. I could have taken the passive route instead, which meant looking at the picture, feeling sorry for myself that I will never again experience the euphoria of doing a difficult climb, and gone on sulking throughout the evening. Not a better choice, right?

Usefully Faulty

In Chapter 2, I promised that we would learn how to put the fallacy of our recollection system to good use; this is it. Do you know how, sometimes, your memory gets mixed up between different events that have some points of contact or similarities? That can be useful in some cases, as it was to me while dealing with this particular exercise. Let me explain. In order to be able to reconstruct a pleasant memory of an event that happened a long time ago, which I cannot for the life of me precisely reconstruct from the limited memory that is buried in my brain, I can get some help from available hard facts and materials not directly related to it. In this example, I did it by using pictures taken on other occasions, during a similar climb—see Appendix B. If you want to make that sound bad, you could say that I purposefully deluded myself by building a false memory, using artifacts that do not belong to the specific event that I was seeking to recall. Some people will surely do that, the naysayers! While they would be factually correct, they would be missing the point. Consider the options: 1) I could have stared at my mountaintop picture for a while, longingly, as it were, trying in vain to feel good about it; or 2) I had the option of jogging my memory (as I did) using suitable props and thus recreating a memory as close as possible to the real one, which, admittedly and necessarily, is grossly inaccurate. Since I *know* that the reconstructed memory is anyway inaccurate, I can make it as pleasant as I want, as long as I don't depart from reasonable boundaries. If I were to reconstruct a memory in which I sprouted wings and flew up to the top, I would feel silly and derive no pleasure whatsoever from it. In order to benefit from the exercise, it had to be as close as possible to my understanding of what actually happened.

Prophylactic Happiness Work
Putting happy memories in perspective so they don't sadden us is important. However, we need to be more proactive in using our imagination if we want to feel happier—we need to count our blessings. Nowadays, I never wait for the blues to catch up with me, as I admit I often did, up to about 10 years ago. Now I do "prophylactic happiness work" by using my free time to both run through great and enjoyable times I had (playing with my grandchildren in my head is one of them) and create active imageries of expected good times to come. It doesn't take me a lot of time: it is often enough for me to do that for 3–5 minutes, to feel energized and in better spirits. At first it may take you longer—15 to 20 minutes—because you need more time to get into the imaginative mindset, but times get shorter quickly as you become experienced.

CHAPTER 7
Imagining for Pleasure and Entertainment

I was fortunate to grow up in a time when social media didn't exist, and a telephone was a big, black thing with a rotating dial, which stood in a corner of our apartment and seldom rang. We were only allowed to watch TV for half an hour in the afternoon, but most of the time there was nothing worth watching. We had much more fun than kids have nowadays: we used our imagination.

You could leave me alone in a silent room with a couple of plastic soldiers, and I would soon make up a story and live a great adventure with them. And role playing was the norm, both with friends and alone. I remember dressing up as a cowboy and spending hours outside chasing the bad guys. Now I see all those young boys and girls, intent on deforming their spines by gazing at their phone screens all day long, and I can't help pitying them. Their imagination has been taken away from them by the modern environment.

But it's never too late to relearn to imagine for pleasure and entertainment.

If we look back at our experience, we can list many occasions when we wished we weren't there or felt stuck in limbo: at the airport, when our flight is delayed, and we forgot to take the book we are reading with us; in class, during a particularly boring lecture; in the dentist's waiting room; and so on. You can easily entertain yourself during any such times, using your imagination. As I said before, imagination is infinite, and you need to make up your own stories, but I will give two examples below:

Aerial View

Think of a scenery with which you are familiar. It doesn't have to be a real one, but some elements of truth will help you to make it feel more real. Better if you can start with a countryside scene. Now elevate your view above that scenery and see the trees or the fields from above. Don't worry about the flying details; it doesn't matter if you got up high using wings or atomic propulsion. Just imagine the view from up there. If you feel the wind on your face as you gently glide above the fields, that's even better.

Now move on toward an inhabited area. Keep gliding above the streets—not too high above, just slightly higher than the rooftops—and zoom in to get a closer look at some details. I like to gaze at beautiful plants through the window of a florist or check out the cakes in the window of a bakery. Realize that you are invisible to the people below. A little innocent voyeurism can be great fun. Innocent, I said! So watching somebody sweating while mowing the lawn can be entertaining, if he is someone we don't particularly like. Allow yourself to be a bit mischievous, in a way that you, a serious person, cannot be in real life.

You get the idea, right? Once you get the hang of it, your imagination will send you where it finds it more interesting and entertaining, and before you know it, the boring lecture will be over.

I have learned to do this with my eyes open, which is really useful if you are being watched. It's an advanced mode that may take some time to learn, but you should try it, eventually. It adds to the fun.

Augmented Recall

I play the piano (I'm not bad at it, really), but I stopped reading musical scores ages ago. Now I play by ear, entirely for my pleasure. It so happens, however, that I may struggle over some particularly difficult piece. One of the things I like to do for entertainment is what I call "augmented recall" (don't bother looking it up; this is another one I have coined, at least in this context[16]), and this is how it works:

I imagine myself playing the piece and running elegantly over the keys when I get to the difficult part. I repeat that a few times without skipping any element of the piece, listening to the music and visualizing the piano, the room, and anything else that comes to my mind, such as the temperature and the scent

---

[16] To my knowledge, this term has been used before in a 1968 paper, but in a different context.

of a nice drink I have prepared before sitting down to play. I use this particular imagery when I have little time to myself, and I know that developing an elaborate imagined scenario is not realistic timewise.

It is a triple win: 1) I fill in dead times easily; 2) I get to enjoy a piece I like; and 3) I end up playing it better when, eventually, I actually get to sit at the piano. This is attributable to the "motor imagery" effect, which is well known in the literature[17] and is capable of creating changes in the neural pathways of our brain. There is ample evidence supporting the positive effect of imagined training to improve actual physical results, for instance in sports requiring concentration, like golf and swimming.

You may not be a pianist, and thus this example may not be for you, but the possibilities are endless, and you can come up with your own. If you want some inspiration and need to see more examples and additional ideas for having fun with your imagination, you can go to my website https://www.doitwithwords.com/htiff or scan the QR code:

---

[17] Hang Zhang et al., **PLoS One.** 2012; 7(5): e36052

CHAPTER 8
Imagining for Problem-Solving

Quite a number of studies have been performed to show that young children (4–5 years old) are capable of using imagination to solve problems,[18] but we, the adults, are no less in need of using it—actually, more so, since our problems are bigger. Sarathy explains[19] that the parts of our brain involved in making

---

[18] April N Kisamore et al., **J Appl Behav Anal.** 2011 Summer; 44(2): 255–278.

[19] Vasanth Sarathy, **Front Hum Neurosci.** 2018; 12: 261.

plans are believed to be activated when recalling past experiences, imagining fictitious and future events and navigating large-scale spaces. The literature contains a lot of big words, but the key words for this discussion are "**imagining fictitious and future events.**" That's how efficient problem solving is done.

One Way to Overcome Problem-Related Anxiety
When I was in elementary school, teachers were scary. *Really* scary. In those ancient times, they had an oral exam you had to pass to be admitted to junior high school, which was supposed to test everything you had learned in the previous five years. Since I had learned very little, I was obviously nervous when the time came to be examined. To make things worse, the examining panel consisted of three professors (that's what they called high-school teachers in those days), whom I had never seen before. They were two moth-eaten males and a female at least 100 years old, or so it seemed to me. Together they made an austere, unsmiling bunch, who sat behind a table in a large, cold, unfriendly room.

We were called to the table alphabetically, so I waited patiently while the pupils before me were being terrorized by those specimens. We were seated at a safe distance, from which we couldn't hear what passed between them, but what we could see was terrifying enough. I had to do something to stop myself from going into full-blown hysterics, and right then I found the solution to my problem. I gazed at the trio. The table hid their bodies entirely below their waist, leaving what was going down below open to my imagination. I started by imagining that the two male professors weren't wearing any pants. Then I pictured them with Mickey Mouse socks, and I made their legs skinny and yellowish. Then I imagined the female professor wearing silk stockings and a pink skirt, with high-heeled shoes. The composition was so hilarious, and in my head they looked so ridiculous, that I was no longer intimidated. I kept improving my imagery, and when my turn came I got to the table, managed to babble a few answers to their questions without fainting, and apparently did reasonably well, because I was admitted to junior high school.

That was my first problem-solving event, in which I made use of my imagination to see me through what at the time looked to me like a terrible ordeal. The problem was that the professors were intimidating, and the solution was to imagine them in a way that changed that cognition.

Structured Problem Solving
Thinking on your feet and imagining on the spot can be a great help if you run into an unexpected problem like I did, but most of the time we struggle with problems for some time before we either come up with a solution or give up (please make a note never to give up). With those types of problems, we need a somewhat more sophisticated approach to imagining. Did you ever happen to go to sleep with an unsolved problem, waking up the next morning with a solution? If you did, you likely allowed your imagination to take you on a multi-option route, where your mind examined the options and picked one. As explained by Arnie Dietrich,[20] creativity can occur as a result of both hard thinking and daydreaming. These processing modes differ in several important ways and support different types of creativity.

Some people (me included) find that a long shower helps in finding solutions to problems, which come to mind either while still under the jet of water or sometime after the shower

---

[20] Arnie Dietrich, ***TEXT Special Issue***, April 2012, http://www.textjournal.com.au/speciss/issue13/Dietrich.pdf

(possibly depending on the length of time in the shower). I have a (fully unproven) theory for it: a shower may have a hypnotic effect, and hypnosis is a great companion to imagination, so if you apply imagination to your problem while in the shower, you get an enhanced result.

It is now generally accepted that unconscious thought is rational[21] and can outperform conscious thought conditions. So now it's time to put two and two together. If working on an issue unconsciously may be better than mulling the problem consciously, then it follows that we need to prime our unconscious mind to work on the problem. And what better way to do so, than applying our imagination, to feed our unconscious mind with scenarios leading up to a solution, in which it has to fill in the blanks? This, of course, is a somewhat simplistic way of describing it, but we don't really need to know more about what our brain does when we ask it to get involved. We only need to know how to create the best conditions for it to get the work done.

A Problem-Solving Procedure
When we come to exploit our imagination in the problem-solving process, we may run into a question: If the process happens unconsciously, then how does actively imagining help with that? Well, it is a bit like cooking a good steak. To do that, you need to light your coals properly, so they burn well and provide homogeneous heat. We can liken our imagination to the lighting stage of the coals. Once we have used our active imagination to put the problem-solving process in motion, our passive imagination, which is steered in the right direction, can do the rest. Our brain uses strong memories—and the more recent, the stronger—as a raw material for the creative process.

---

[21] Katie E. Garrison and Ian M. Handley, **Front. Psychol.**, 06 July 2017

Imagining creates inherently strong, recent memories, which can be used for creativity, including problem solving, by our passive imagination.

So this is what you do: Start by imagining yourself dealing with the problem (not ruminating about it). Here is an example: If your problem is that you need to get somewhere at a given time, and you can't see how to do it because your car is at the shop for maintenance, start imagining yourself getting to your destination in time. If you want, you can let your imagination go wild a bit, so you get there by boat or airplane. Make the decision that you will definitely get there, and then stop thinking about it, go for a walk, or take a shower or a nap, to let your mind do the rest. While you imagine, it is useful to think of several different situations, even those that seem not to be available or realistic at the time. You are feeding your mind information that it can use to reach the goal you have put to it.

This is admittedly a simplistic (and rather unrealistic) example, but it serves to illustrate the steps you need to take. These are quite simple: Make a decision that you are going to solve the problem, imagine yourself solving it in as many ways as you can think of, and let your mind do the rest. I can't promise that you will be able to solve every problem in this way, because some problems are unsolvable, and some goals are unrealistic. But for the run-of-the-mill problem, this approach works well much of the time.

Using our imagination to approach a problem is much less stressful than putting our mind to it compulsively, which often obtains the opposite effect, so we end up feeling empty-headed. It's a "softer" way to go about it, and you will find it more effective than many highly structured problem-solving strategies. Forget charts, plans, and data, for a moment, and give yourself a chance to do it more naturally. You may be surprised by the result.

CHAPTER 9
Imagining For Creativity

"Imagination is more important than knowledge. Knowledge is limited. Imagination encircles the world."
—— **Albert Einstein**

"Leave the beaten track behind occasionally and dive into the woods. Every time you do, you will be certain to find something you have never seen before."
—— **Alexander Graham Bell**

Creativity and problem solving are related but are treated separately here because we are more interested in the result than in the mechanism that brings it about. The fact that you need to be imaginative to be creative is a given. Unless you can imagine something out of the ordinary to take shape or happen, it will never come into being. But "being imaginative" is not the same as "using our imagination." One can be imaginative simply by looking at something and seeing it as it should become. Architects think of a concept for a building and play with it on paper, going through different versions until they are satisfied. The resulting idea may be greatly imaginative, but they don't close their eyes for five minutes and watch the building sprout from the ground (at least not the ones I have spoken with).

Many studies have confirmed the correlation between the ability to imagine and manipulate visual elements[22] and creativity. However, these studies concentrate on static imagery, probably because they are easier to study in a scientific environment. Luckily, we can take from scientific research what is useful to us in our quest for a better quality of life, without feeling obliged to apply rigorous scientific methods, as long as what we do works well for us.

Unless you are five years old (in which case please get back to me in 15 years or so), you have accumulated a lot of information that you don't use on a daily basis. The trick is to exploit those pieces of information as if they were the building blocks of a game, which you can use to build a house or a giraffe, depending on the way in which you assemble them. Let's take an example.

---

[22] Maddalena Boccia et al., **Front Psychol.** 2015; 6: 1195

Creating the House of Your Dreams

Your rich uncle left you enough money to build the house of your dreams. You have been to many country houses that you found charming, each one in its own way. You liked the library in that one, the porch in the other, the fireplace in another, and so on, but you never saw a house just like you wanted. Now you have to get a clear idea of what your house will look like. You have two options:

Option 1: You can buy a few architecture books, look at old photos, and get a few journals together and then sit with your architect to point out to him the features you like in this or that picture, or ...

Option 2: You can close your eyes, lean back in your armchair (a good drink is optional but recommended), and start walking through your dream house. Start with the entrance, with that stairway that is almost like those you saw once, only better, and then walk through the rooms, noting the windows that let a lot of light in and also the pictures on the walls. Those prints of ducks that you have in the corridor (you always liked prints) look right in their place. You can walk down to the ground floor and then go up again, to find the rooms disposed slightly differently, and you can do that until they feel absolutely right to you. Then it's time to go out and sit on the porch in that rocking chair you always wanted and never had room for.

Which of the options will end up allowing you to describe the true house of your dreams to your architect? I guess you know the answer.

Putting Words Together

Imagination and creativity go hand in hand not only with physical things like a house. If you have a difficult letter to write or a delicate talk to have with someone, playing those in your head, along with the way in which you see the other person reacting to them, is sure to help you write the better letter, or approach a thorny subject in the most appropriate way for the person with whom you need to discuss it. In these cases it has to do with empathy—the ability to put yourself in the other person's shoes, which is greatly enhanced through active imagination.

Imagination allows us to test a great number of alternative situations and outcomes in a painless, cost-free way. Those who don't know how to exploit it are doomed to choose trite, formulaic solutions that can be summoned to mind with a simple, static image. If you have read this far, obviously you don't want to be that person.

CHAPTER 10
The Fear of Imagination

If you surf the web searching for "fear" and "imagination" you will find many posts and articles wondering whether imagining can increase our anxiety and fears. I have two answers to that: 1) yes it can, if you do it wrong; and 2) don't google that.

Children have fears, and the more intelligent the child, the more ridden with anxiety and fears he or she is. Does that mean that we want our children to be dumb so they won't feel fear? I guess not. More intelligent children have a more developed imagination, and they often imagine so well that they are incapable of distinguishing imagination from reality. There is little we can do, other than reassuring them when needed, but I would certainly not choose to stifle a child's imagination.

I have brought up passive imagination before and its different meaning from active imagination. Passive imagination is when a thought pops up in our mind, and we let it take over and start a train of thought that is bad for us. Our mind likes to play those tricks on us, and, left to itself, it will sometimes be really mean to us. The solution, as I said before, is active imagination. When you apply active imagination, you are in control. You are the scriptwriter and the director of your movie, and you don't let the script take you where you don't want to go. You can give it some slack, but you need to keep it on a leash and pull it back if it looks like taking a wrong turn.

Stopping Imagined Fear
Active imagination is what helps you to stop imagined fear. When you are anxious and a bad thought pops up in your mind, you can use your active imagination to hijack it and stop the fear from developing. Take, for example, fear of flying. Flights can be a bit bumpy at times, and if you are plagued with fear of flying, each time you feel a little turbulence you start imagining the plane going down, possibly using a clip from some aerial disaster movie you have seen. As soon as you realize that this is happening, you need to take control of the movie that runs in your head. You can do this in two ways:

Option 1: If you are good at imagining and have some strong imagery ready, substitute the image of the plane about to crash into the ocean with your strong imagery. For instance, if you like skiing, see yourself gliding down a slope, better if it is one you actually did, and run with it, creating a movie as long as you need to forget about the plane.

Option 2: You can do the opposite, staying with the plane but taking control of it. See it from the outside, flying peacefully and note the turbulence and the fact that even if it shakes the plane a little, nothing happens to it. See the plane flying safely toward good weather and realize how unimportant a little turbulence is.

This process can be applied to any kind of fear or anxiety. The trick is to substitute the perception of your current situation with a movie in your head, which will keep you busy until the worry is gone. It is not unlike the method proposed in Chapter 6, for dealing with "the blues," and, in fact, the methodology is the same.

Testing New Situations

Are you familiar with that nagging feeling, in the back of your mind, that something in your future is bothering you? Maybe you have to do something you never did before, like taking a medical test or going on a tour involving a funicular that doesn't look too safe to you. You are likely to do all you can to push it away from your consciousness, each time it pops into your head. That is probably the wrong thing to do.

Using your imagination to pre-test situations may be useful to assuage your fear or discomfort at the thought of what's coming. Instead of being in denial until the last moment that the event you dread is going to happen, you can use your imagination to test yourself and your reaction to it, explore various angles of it, and possibly stop demonizing it.

As Jo Marchant explains,[23] warning patients about pain or discomfort they are about to feel is a staple of conventional medical care. But during medical procedures such as scans or operations, we are particularly susceptible to the nocebo effect, and being told how much things are about to hurt simply worsens our pain. Similarly, pushing the thought of what you have to do into a corner of your mind does pretty much the same, because you can't help thinking, even if only for a second, that "it's going to hurt," or "I'm going to panic on that funicular." Using your imagination to rationally pre-test the situation may go a long way toward reducing your level of anxiety and allowing you to perform better when you actually have to deal with whatever situation you need to face.

Avoiding Overdoing It
Imagination is great but can be addictive. Because living in an imagined world or situation may be much more pleasant than our real one, someone may be tempted to spend too much time in a fantasy. In extreme cases one may become unable to distinguish between reality and fantasy. That's why, like with everything else in life, we must make use of our active imagination in a sensible way. We must not be tempted to use it to escape reality for the sake of avoiding coping with a problem that must be confronted—on the contrary, we must use it to help us cope with whatever unpleasant situation we are facing. Using imagination to distract us, as for example when confronting a panic attack during a flight, does not mean that we are departing from reality; it means that, for a time, we are concentrating on a different, more wholesome subject. And if

---

[23] Marchant, Jo., ***Cure: A Journey into the Science of Mind Over Body***. Crown/Archetype.

we are imagining just for pleasure, we must limit ourselves to short stints into our active imagination, pretty much like we don't drink too much and don't overdose on chocolate.

Not everybody knows it, but too much water—the most important and innocuous of molecules—is deadly (it may lead to an electrolyte imbalance that can cause death). The conclusion is that anything taken or used in excess may have negative results. The Internet and computer games are other examples, because they may absorb the player to a point where the border between reality and the game is no longer clear.

Another issue that people worry about is whether allowing ourselves to imagine may not bring up troubling thoughts, experiences, or memories that we have hidden deep inside. That cannot be ruled out, if you follow an imagery that may take you there. Psychiatrists use guided imagery to bring troubling memories to the surface, the idea being to deal with the issue and bring it to a resolution. Good for them, but this is not what this book is about. Deep, introspective soul-searching is off limits, as far as this discussion is concerned. We want to enjoy our imagination, have fun with it, and use it to chase away bad moods, but we are not planning to start digging into the meanders of our psyche.

As I have said a few times already, you are the captain, the director, the scriptwriter, and you decide where to go when you spend time actively imagining. If you feel the temptation to become all deep and profound and search for the meaning of life, please kick that temptation in the groin and see yourself on the beach with a good martini instead. And if you plan to go on a DIY journey to uncover some deeply hidden childhood trauma, stop right there and talk to a health practitioner about it.

CHAPTER 11
Conclusion

As you know by now, imagination is a multi-faceted subject that can fill many thick tomes of highly scientific discussions, some of which may even be valuable. However, you (and any other right-minded person) are not likely to find the time or the interest to read hundreds and thousands of pages. So here's what have we learned up to now:

- We have discussed the link between imagination and memory and how to work with both of them to feel happier.

- We have identified times when using active imagination fetches the best results with the least effort.

- We have seen how to use our imagination while working on our dreams.

- We have discovered that we can use our imagination to entertain ourselves, help us solve problems, enhance our creativity, and dispel our fears.

Not a bad harvest for a guide that is short, practical, and completely void of frills, I would say.

Active imagination may not appeal to everybody, but if it does to you, I believe that this book has fulfilled its role of giving you a gentle push in the right direction, and you can start to enjoy daydreaming.

The great thing about imagining is that nobody can tell you what to do while you do it. You are the master, and you are in absolute control of the What, When, and How. The question that we need to pose to ourselves is, "What is the most problematic roadblock that needs to be removed, to empower us to enjoy active imagination?" The answer to that question is easy: shame.

We are serious adults (at least, until proven otherwise), who are not comfortable behaving childishly. Engaging in make believe, making up stories, and having fun with them, is something that we may feel shame doing. We would not go to our employer and tell him or her that our phone was off the hook because we were busy imagining ourselves water-surfing in anticipation of next week's vacation. We would not admit to anybody that sometimes we "make things up," for fear of being considered unbalanced. But here's the thing: Nobody needs to know what you daydream.

Still, there is a stigma associated with dreamy behavior, which blocks some people from pursuing active imagination even in the privacy of their mind. So we needed to air the subject, show that the stigma is silly, and remove it. I hope I have convinced you of the value of active imagination and given you some ideas that will help you to explore your imaginative abilities. We need to remember that, as Sir James Crichton Browne aptly said, **those who know how to revel in imagination are the healthy minded.** The insane are the least imaginative of beings, the lunatic is as dull as a stone, and idiocy is the absolute negation of imagination. I hope you won't let the idiots dictate how happy you can feel on any given day.

And if I have helped you to realize that, my work here is done.

Meet the Author:

Kfir Luzzatto is the author of eleven novels, several short stories and seven non-fiction books. Kfir was born and raised in Italy, and moved to Israel as a teenager. He acquired the love for the English language from his father, a former U.S. soldier, a voracious reader, and a prolific writer. He holds a PhD in chemical engineering and works as a patent attorney. In pursuit of his interest in the mind-body connection, Kfir was certified as a Clinical Hypnotherapist by the Anglo European College of Therapeutic Hypnosis.

Kfir is an HWA (Horror Writers Association) and ITW (International Thriller Writers) member. You can visit Kfir's web site and read his blog at https://www.kfirluzzatto.com. Follow him on Twitter (@KfirLuzzatto) and friend him on Facebook (https://www.facebook.com/KfirLuzzattoAuthor)

Other Non-Fiction Books by Kfir Luzzatto

HOW TO REVERSE YOUR DIABETES (If You Really Mean It)

BEWARE OF YOUR DOCTOR: How to Survive the Medical System

THE SECRET LIFE OF YOUR BLOOD SUGAR: A Diabetes Skeleton in Your Doctor's Closet

THINK AWAY YOUR HAY FEVER: A Practical Guide

DO IT WITH WORDS: Regrow Your Hair with Your Mind

FUN WITH PATENTS: The Irreverent Guide for the Investor, the Entrepreneur, and the Inventor

Appendix A
The Pleasures of Imagination Defended, 1889

354 **THE HOSPITAL.** **September 7, 1889.**

is such a brain and nerve tonic as all the chemists' laboratories in the world cannot produce the equal of. Nothing locks the door of memory and bars it so fast and tight as honest work well done. Let a man give his soul to his work, let him find his pleasure in it, let him do it for its own sake, and stand to it until it is completed and finished, and he will not, as a rule, be troubled with ghosts at midnight who "murder sleep" and "urge to madness the despairing soul." "Let the dead bury their dead," said the greatest of all teachers. Let the paralysing memories of the past be driven away and forgotten. Present time and strength are for present duty, and present duty done brings present reward of mental wholesomeness and physical health.

THE PLEASURES OF IMAGINATION DEFENDED.

THE scientific uses of the imagination have been ere this the theme of the philosopher, and its abuses the subject of the sermon of the preacher, but never before have so many brilliant things been said in defence of the powers and pleasures of imagination as by Sir James Crichton Browne in his address to the British Medical Association, which has just met at Leeds. "All true science rests on imaginings," he boldly asserts, and this statement he elucidates by showing how imagination's help is called in to supply scientific men with speculations and hypotheses, to trace disease to its source, and to arrange, combine, and co-ordinate the isolated facts of knowledge. But besides availing themselves of the uses, Sir Crichton urges his medical brethren to enjoy the pleasures of the imagination, and to "ramble for a little in the green pastures of literature or climb the pinnacles of art." He looks on undismayed at the growing taste for the literature of fiction, as shown by the returns from the lending libraries, inasmuch as he asserts that as men become more educated the influence of tales of horror and crime is not to be dreaded; for it is only the ignorant and neglected boy, keen, perhaps, with that superficial sharpness that is really a kind of imbecility, but with a narrow intellectual horizon, that is lured into wickedness by the penny dreadfuls; and the silly and dissipated youths of better social position who go to ruin can rarely trace their downfall to poetry or fiction; while to the healthy minded, imaginative literature may heighten happiness, afford solace in suffering and sorrow, give brace to exertion, and lessen the sense of fatigue. It is a mistake, Sir Crichton asserts, to think that indulging in the pleasures of imagination induces insanity, for "for one case of insanity caused by excess of imagination there are a dozen caused by want of it." The insane are the least imaginative of beings, the lunatic is as dull as a stone, and idiocy is the absolute negation of imagination. One of the most valuable aids in the treatment of the insane is the imagination, which is invoked in every possible way, by music, pictures, and the drama in all lunatic asylums worthy of the name, and the first recorded case of the cure of melancholia was by the harp of David. Religion, which the Bishop of Ripon said had been accused of being "the nurse of hysteria and the mother of hallucinations," Sir Crichton Browne declares "to make for sanity," by affording support under sorrow and misfortune, maintaining mental equilibrium in agitating times, and supplying lofty motives to conduct, and so cleansing and controlling life; but on faith-healers and the "peculiar people" the orator pours his sarcasm, and calls upon them to learn how to make an accurate clinical report, and to apprehend what induction means, before assertin the cure of diseases which were simulated, or which ran a natural course or were purely subjective. Here is an example of imagination run wild, but its normal use in the economy might be spoken of as that of a pioneer opening up new pathways in the brain, or as a mode of transit between its territories. The brain that is without imagination is like a country without roads or railways, in which locomotion is laborious and slow; and the brain richly gifted with it is like one in which steam and electricity have established easy and rapid communications. "If," as Matthew Arnold says, "two-thirds of life are conduct," it may truly be alleged that three-fourths of thought are imagination. It is not merely the child who builds castles in the air. Each of us—the most matter-of-fact as well as the most romantic—has "cloud-capped palaces and gorgeous towers," known to himself alone, to which, in hours of solitude and reverie, or sadness and chagrin, he retires with ever-renewed wonder and exaltation, and from which he scatters beneficence on all around. And the great faculty that out of thin air constructs these cities of refuge for us, and enables us, in a sense, to shape our own environments, is the handmaid of science, the giver of insight, and the harmoniser of discords.

We must add our grateful thanks to Sir Crichton Browne for a defence so eloquent and scientific of one of the greatest pleasures of life.

Appendix B
Using Still Images to Recreate a Movie

Your imagination is your "engine," and it needs "fuel" to work. In the example given in Chapter 6, I used these images of me, taken on two different occasions, to recreate the climb done on a third occasion:

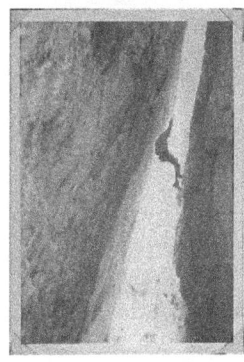

www.ingramcontent.com/pod-product-compliance
Lightning Source LLC
Chambersburg PA
CBHW051702040426
42446CB00009B/1257